A river of Gratitude

In early spring, I asked ten friends to read a poem of mine every day for six weeks and rate each one on a five star scale from cold to boiling. I was blessed day in and day out by their honest responses and steadfast participation. My gratitude flows to Nadine Aiello, Steve Bollock, Rebecca Evert, Andrea Freeman, Mark Gardiner, Clare Morris, Larry Robinson, Maya Spector, Jean Sward and George Taylor. I award each of them six stars on a five star scale. Please be kind to them, the final call for a poem inclusion was mine alone.

And more stars and praise to Nadine Aiello Graphics for their artistic support and limitless patience in the creation of Gratitude Goulash.

And finally as my raft meanders down the endless river of gratitude, notice who else is aboard... All my friends of The Minnesota Men's Conference, The Great Mother and New Father Conference, The Redwood Men's Center Conference, The Hepwa Men's Council, Rumi's Caravan and The Noah Project. Thank you for keeping me afloat through the rapids.

Doug von Koss

Poems

Stuff

Poems

TRUE NORTH

That other compass
    you bought in the city
        is no good to you now

Before darkness comes
    give it away

Pause in your confusion

Stand quiet in the fading light
    Say, I am lost.
        Say, Where is my life waiting?
        Say, I want an answer!

Then, in the gathering dusk
    some quiet part of you
        may begin to open

Call it your inner compass rose

Call it the home of your true north
    as constant as Polaris
        in the night sky

If there is an aroma
    faint in the evening breeze
        take a grateful breath and
            move in that direction

Your road will be there,
    glowing in the moonlight

Say, Thank you for this unfolding

Your compass rose has opened

MORNING LESSON - OAKRIDGE TENNESSEE

In the pink dogwoods
>   above this man-made pond on
>   Black Oak Ridge
>   cardinals flash their brilliant red
>   while water born miracles
>   play and pray in the sunlight

No fear or shame nothing hidden or concealed
>   majestically the koi are being themselves
>   no pretense in the morning light

The golden fish are what they are
>   koi being perfectly koi
>   silvery gold and yellowy white
>   angel wing fins and
>   tails like shimmering fans
>   each unique and divine

They glide and turn in
>   a sensuous dance
>   among the lily pads
>   in the quiet pond

In the ripples the teaching is clear

Just be

Just be

THE GAZE

The reverence of gaze, I heard him say

The words caught me
Reverence
Gaze
Have I ever done that
Can I do that

Looking as if to see God,
in the object
in the thing

In the yellow and green caterpillar sneaking
across the top of this page

Do we catch our Gods in paintings and books
or in mid-flight or mid-bloom
or in sublime repose
in a patch of sun

Can I gaze with enough reverence
to see a God
in the object
in the thing

In the slowly opening fingers of the homeless
woman's dirty and twisted hand

Reverence of gaze?

God help me

>   August 17, 2002 after an evening
>   with John O'Donohue

Sadly We Are One

The push the pull
the burgundy wool
must be just so
on the monk's robe

Rework a fold
the sash retied
a wrinkle smoothed
but nothing hides
the tired body
the sad smile
of the man
with a shaved head
and a dark voice
who knows --

Karma is not the same
as destiny
and everything is
One's self.

Who knows
we are one
all are one
we are all one

Yet if we love another and part forever
we will suffer

His sad eyes close
chin falls
burgundy robe
drapes and flows

Namaste
Sadly we are one

THE PEOPLE'S CIRCLES

High above the roiling Klamath River
quiet meditation under a black oak tree
my mind circles what once was

A grinding stone remains half buried
an everyday tool left behind
where acorns continue to fall

How long have they been gone

My hand rests on a massive river stone
carried here by strong people
to make a circular stone foundation
to form a circular shelter
to create a circular village
to live a circular life
under the circles of eagle and osprey
under the circles of sun and moon

Time circles the place I sit
near the fragmenting edge of
a huge bowl shaped crater

The forest and all its living things
continue their circle making
covering and concealing
taking back to the earth
the last remains
the crumbling work
of generations of The People

...

...
Scooped circles in the earth
      and heavy stones
      all that mark their passing

One day, the stones too
      will join the circle
Even now, circular tears
      join the circle

६ 6

Water Kisses

The boat of my interior life
allowed its own meander
floats upstream in eddies
of a lingering calm memory

A water drop released above me
falling from the uncurling fern
growing from the steep hillside
in the shelter of clinging laurels
where the river kissed
the banks of the Klamath River

Washed awake from bird song dreams
pulled unwillingly to a new day
by a single drop of
icy morning dew

The dew dropping
trickled into the tiny cup
where my eye meets my nose
then my eyes met the river

My lord what a morning

Snow Talk

So I said, I don't have a poem about snow
but maybe Snow, you got a poem about me?

So Snow said, You? You who hide out from me
in your always green, never freeze, home by the bay?

So I said, Hey, lighten up! You're the first snow I've
seen in a long, long time. You caught me by surprise.
Suddenly everything white over-night you know?

With an attitude that shocked me, Snow said,
What's wrong with white,
great overwhelming vistas of white?
White upon white 'til you pray
for a touch of brown or blue!
But not today buddy, no not today!
Today you are mine, all mine
at fifty-five hundred feet.

Look at me. Am I not beautiful?
Do I not take your breath away
doing what I do?

I am snow.
Perfectly impartial to all who know me
Yes, even to you who avoid me.
I am snow and
I am beautiful.

Mt. Shasta, CA   October 2010

&8

Mountain Lion

Why should we be surprised to find
a mountain lion on a mountain
that's where they live
that's why the name
 Mountain Lion

Cites have their slickers
the country has its bumpkins
villages have their idiots
and mountains have their lions

They are called mountain lions
not valley lions or prairie lions

Mountain Lions
and they were there first

So in lion country on your mountain bike
best be a mountain man
or mountain woman
or a Mountain Lion may eat
your candy ass for lunch

> San Francisco 2003
> Response to surprised off road
> bicycle enthusiasts

89

TURTLE MEDICINE

The Royal Order of Turtles is convened
        in San Francisco
        in my small house

Turtles fly in from Japan
        enter through the mail slot
        hide in my suitcase from a trip to New Orleans
        crawl in from Arizona
        why last night Turtle came in a dream

The first one arrived as a gift
        and took pride of place
        on my desk
        a surprisingly heavy
        cast iron turtle with
        a hinged back

His empty belly a perfect place to hide
        a Buffalo Nickel, a kernel of corn
        and once mysteriously
        a totally secret wish
        stashed beneath the shell
        vanished without a trace

Old Cast Iron was the first, a scout I think and now
        his entire tribe has set up camp
        twenty nine in the house
        three hibernating in the garden
        and more arriving every day

        ...

...

On the wall behind the guest room door
       how he got there I don't know
       a purple desert tortoise
       with a jaundiced eye
       passes judgement on me
       beneath his personal Joshua tree

Perched on the windowsill of my cluttered study
       never complaining
       a white marble turtle struggles to the baths
       a fat Roman Senator on his back

And I can't forget the beaded back
       Quichol turtle from Yalapa
       who danced when the radio played
       mariachi music on Cinco de Mayo

All attempts to reduce the herd have failed
       they won't leave willingly
       so we've worked out a shared economy
       of space

They haven't changed but I have
       sticking my neck out in this crowd
       is a thing of the past
       and yes, I don't hurry anywhere
       troubles, big and small
       now easily roll off my back
       ...

...

Turtle has done his work
        lifted my hinged back
        placed something there
        of his choosing

Perhaps a medicine of some kind
        greet one turtle
        first thing on arising
        for the rest of your days

Hmmm, and so I shall

CHICKEN LITTLE INTERNATIONAL AIRPORT

Your attention please in Terminal One

This is an "Oh, my God, the sky is falling" alert
If the sky falls of course, all flights will
    be permanently delayed

This facility and our precious sky are now
    at Mandarin orange rapidly
    heading to vermillion
We at Homeland Security are hopeful for a return
    to Mother Teresa Blue
    with perhaps just a touch of
    Mahatma Gandhi white

Please turn off all electronic devices
    Toshibas, Nokias, Sonys and Blackberries
    and IPads, and IPhones and Aye yi yi…
Technology will *not* save us

With this announcement, all meditators
    in all terminals throughout California
    are being activated

This is not a test
    If it were a test
    we would activate Fairfield, Iowa
    or Fargo, North Dakota

Homeland security has requested
    all those who meditate
    particularly the transcendentalists
    proceed to your boarding gate
    and return to your spiritual practice

…

& 13

...
If you have forgotten your mantra, no shame
Proceed to a white courtesy telephone
 Speak clearly into the phone
 Maharishi Mahesh Yogi,
 Paramahansa Yogananda,
 Thich Nhat Hanh
 Shakyamuni Buddha
 or Jai Guru Dev

A temporary mantra will be issued to you
on a need to know basis. Do not share it
Your mantra may be dangerous to others

You who meditate, this is the moment
 you have waited for
 and quietly questioned
Can a calm and centered community really
 hold up things that are falling around them

What if this stuff doesn't work as advertised

We'll have the answers soon
 as you take to the unfriendly skies

Once you begin again, do not stop
Your practice must continue throughout
 the boarding process and for the duration
 of your flight in this life

You can do this -- you know you can
 Hold up our sky, yours and mine
...

...
Forget your perfect posture
　or the cushion you left at home
Remember Gandhi White
Remember Mother Teresa blue

All together now -- Three deep breaths
　Inhale Los Angeles, exhale Yellowstone
　Inhale Washington, DC, exhale Lake Tahoe

Your flight is about to board
Have a nice day

　　　San Francisco International Airport
　　　May 2010

DEPORTATION

Well it's happened
      I'm being deported

They came last week
      a pair of suits with attitude
They're sending me back
      to where I came from --
      Davenport, Iowa

Somebody snitched
      I wasn't born in California
The State Water Conservation and Immigration Service
      were on the job and in my face
Did I have identification
      We soon agreed that I was
      who I thought I was

Sir, the tall one said, you have one week
      I couldn't believe it

      I haven't washed my car in seven months

Sir, he said, you're drinking our water
      He had me there

You have to leave
      But I don't know anyone in Iowa
      I haven't spoken Iowanese in 60 years
...

...
You can learn it again
>   *I'm a Democrat for Cripes sake*

Do you have a green card
>   *I'm retired*

Do you have an immigrant visa
>   *I have a Visa card*

Use it to buy a bus ticket
>   *But this is my home*

Not anymore
>   *I know I wasn't born here*

You admit it then
>   *But I got here as soon as I could*

The short guy said, do you speak any Iowanese
>   *Just please, thank you and I didn't do it*

Sir, you won't have any trouble in Iowa

They left and I thought about it
>   *I'll show them*
Before I leave California
>   *I'll take a long shower
>   and wash my car*

>   Year of the drought 2015

&17

Morning Report On My Immigrant Clothing

Awakened wearing old and faded
Calvin Klein sleepwear Made in Kenya
After the shower my made in the USA body
dried by a Martha Stewart towel Made in India
Warmed by my East Coast L.L. Bean bathrobe
from El Salvador

I made my coffee with beans gathered from
God knows where

Pulling on clothes, still curious and not surprised,
striped Perry Ellis boxers Made in China and jeez
my iconic American Carhartt Jeans started in Nicaragua

And what's more American than a T-shirt?
Not my Made in Peru pepper green "T"
from Territory Ahead
And who knows where my socks started,
maybe Bangalore
My shabby running shoes let into the country by Adidas,
probably began jogging in Northern India

So I'm almost ready and grab my hat. Now wait for it
My trouble making, eye catching, brilliant red,
Human Rights Campaign hat emblazoned
"Make America Gay Again"
was made in the USA

If they send my clothes back with the immigrants
I won't be naked

&18

Any News

The black bird on the bent tower
where the windmill used to turn
on that deserted farm in Illinois
is still waiting in the falling rain
for any news, any sign
that tomorrow
might be better

My Black Wing

My Black wing is one of a pair
a pair of great black wings
I keep concealed under red shirts or yellow coats
and all things bright and beautiful

Only when it is so dark
even the night cries out for light
I drop the covering, the concealment

I reveal the hidden and my dark wings
open further and further until
the slightest breeze ripples their feathers
then moving forward, just the slightest
move forward and I am airborne

Airborne over stagnant and fetid ponds
the dead forests, the national military
cemeteries stretching for miles
over the grieving fathers and mothers of
children dead from senseless killings

I fly on my great black wings over the NRA
National Headquarters and cry havoc on
their rifles of assault

My wings carry me over Washington, DC
shedding black feathers on the houses of
congress, glide over the memorials to men
and women who have died for freedoms
held hostage by guns. Fly gently above
the graves of black men and women killed
because they were black
...

&20

...
I shed black tears as I remember
the slaughter of innocent children, dead
because Mom or Dad thought they needed
a gun in their car or their purse

My red blood turns black
black with sorrow and rage
and my great black wings
will never end their flight

TWIN SONS

Twin sons I am
     of Turquoise Man
Hand-on-fire I am
     and Honey-of-water-flower I am
Twin sons I am
     of Turquoise Man

Strength of bear jaws I have
     Hand-on-fire I am
Power of woven patterns I have
     Honey-of-water-flower I am
Twin sons I am
     Of Turquoise Man

     Together we walk
     Together we rest
     Together we dream
     Together we hunt

Turquoise Man my father is

Twin sons of Turquoise Man I am
     Hand-on-fire I am
     Honey-of-water-flower I am

Twin sons of Turquoise Man I am

IOWA, winter in town, 1941

From the hot grate on the kitchen floor
furnace heat flows up my flannel pajamas
when you're nine, it's a boon

Heard every school morning from our own
Philco Cathedral radio on the shelf that Dad built
Don McNiell, all the way from Chicago, calls out
"second call to breakfast, Philco's call to breakfast"
boon number two

Quaker oatmeal bubbling at my elbow on the big burner
of the Tappan stove with the always wrong clock
I stand ready with the full cup of Sun-Maid raisins
boon number three

Colgate brushless shaving cream and Old Spice
Dad shaving at the kitchen sink
his joyous off key singing
Is that the Chattanooga Choo Choo
boon number four

Hand me a towel, he says, not that one
with the chicken, that one with the stripe
no boon, no harm

The mismatched oak chairs
this time painted a sea-mist puke green
crowd around the way too big table
in the too small Iowa kitchen
No harm

...

...
And much too close to my nine year old nose
though Mom scrubbed the table three times a day
the oil cloth from Woolworth's basement
purple with yellow peaches and red cherries
smelling of linseed oil
winter and summer
never stopped stinking

PLEASE DISTURB

I hung out my "please disturb sign"
      but nobody did

It would have been fine with me

Nobody reads anymore
      it's all this television

So I stayed on my side of the door
      nobody even knocked

It was a nice looking door

Then one morning the maid knocked
      She didn't bother to read my special sign

I yelled, "Come in, oh God, please come in!"
      She said, "I'll come back."

Nobody reads anymore

      After five days at the Royal York Hotel
      Toronto, Canada. May 25, 1994

THE INCISION

Here we go, said the beautiful young nurse
You are now gently sedated
You'll be awake throughout
I hear this with a tranquilized befuddled brain

Nice job with the razors last night sir
but you missed a few in the crease
I mumble, Crease?
The crease between your thigh and your balls sir
I'll just get them now, she says

Oh, God! Dignity? Modesty? My balls?
I'm a body at the mercy of strangers
I seem to wake in a room full of T-V's
glaring lights and an army in blue pajamas

They must have made the cut. I swear
something is crawling up an unknown channel
above the stomach and below the ribs

Ah, jeez, is it stuck? You feel a wiggle
in the groin and near the heart
The heart. This is what it's about
The blue people are near my heart

What did he say? Get ready for what?
Heat? A flush? What the hell?
Oh, God I am hot, head to toe I'm hot
and I know they are at my heart
...

...
Keep breathing. I'm cooling down
What's with the numbers?
Will a 24N43 or a 297B do the job?
Christ. Are they having a math problem?
No. They're talking about the stent
Oh-oh! They're at the crease again

Following the tube is easier this time
There is something new pushing up the river
I swear I feel the nudge and a gentle touch
These guys are on my heart
Not - near - but - on - my - heart

Sudden silence in the white room
Is this it? The big good-bye?
But it is not.
Someone mumbles something
The tube goes back down the river

Someone says, "Good job everybody."
A blue person wheels me out and life goes on
Now what?

August 2011

SITUATION WANTED

Unemployed lover needs job
84 years experience
Unexpectedly laid off by the universe
References destroyed by flood of tears
Can re-locate heart to new location
Will show up every day
Rain or shine
Internship not acceptable
Call 1-800-LOVER

Kissing Nick Good-bye

It could have happened anywhere
 like at his home in New York City
  or my home in San Francisco.
   or in any park beneath any tree

Nick kissed me
 Well, I kissed him back
  but he started it

A long, hot, take-no-prisoners kiss
 a Zeus meets Ganymede moment
  in the ever so romantic
   Portland, Maine Airport

Nick of the black tangling hair curling
 mustache and the D'Artagnan boots
Nick of the high cheek bones
 flushed a desert rose
  pants rolled and cuffed above the boots
   standing there a pirate, a musketeer
Nick, a handsome, radiant, glowing youth
 exuding a fragrance from the sea-side
  of old Carthage

He was a drive-by love bomb

What could we do
 what would you do
  while standing at gate number two
   in a maddening crowd of travelers
...

...
We kissed
    then we kissed
        one for the road

When a love bomb explodes, you have to kiss

Then one last kiss so we both would know
    it could happen and it really did

June 10, 2012 Portland, Maine

& 30

Ode To That Green Harmonica

Oh, how you made my heart weep
    that full moon night in the mountain pines
    your sound crying the tears
    of hundreds of blues players
    wailing their losses to the night
    and the distant stars

Your sound carried enough loneliness
    to make the heavens moan
    and rain for months

Your shine worn down by sliding hands --
    hands easing out low breathy shimmers
    caressing the empty places, the shattered dreams
    of lonely sweethearts
    weeping in the night

I pick you up like the sensuous treasure
    you are - and gently kiss
    your lips

You ask only my breath
    my simple breath
    that makes you nearly shiver
    out of my hands

You are full to bursting
    with sorrowful blues
    falling in the darkness
    ...

...
Your sound calls in the love sick
  cowboy and the tired cook
  the railroad man too tired to go to bed
  the little child too alive
  to go to sleep while your sound
  still curls in his ears

With all your sad moans
  your green is still the greenest green
  that ever a harmonica was - let someone else
  try to find a greener green
  than you

That's it! You beautiful green harmonica
That's it!

Maybe you once were black
  with all the sorrows of the world
  perhaps those tiny holes
  like sand through a sieve
  filtered out the hurtful parts

You took only the honeyed leavings
  of bleeding passion
  and eased them into the air

  And the trees heard

Yes, they heard and gave you back
  their beauty, their greenest green
  of praising spring

Oh, you beautiful green harmonica!
Oh! Oh! Oh-hh!

Mat's Guitar

Sometimes when I hear
        the sad single strings
        of a Spanish guitar
        played by a man alone
        in an old rhythm
        that wandered far
        from its home in Andalusia

My heart fills to bursting
        with a sweet pain
        a glorious sadness
        a grief so immense

I could not eat it all
        if I had a thousand
        lonely Sunday mornings

THE NIGHT SHE DANCED

A smoky basement in Seville
     cigar plumes hanging low
     a single bulb with a bent green shade
      lights it all

Underneath the singer's bleeding voice
     ancient rhythms throbbed
     from an old guitar and there
     near the bottom step
     something dark leaned
     against the wall

It was then Delilia swirled her skirt
     and danced and danced
     on the pitted mahogany floor
     danced the whole history of Andalusia
     out of the night and
     into the room

All those times of exquisite pain
     and painful joy
Like the night the grandmother died
     and the grandchild was born in Favencia
and that year that the Guadalimar
     leaped from its banks and carried away
     the lemon orchard and the mule
the time the bull with the broken horn
     crashed through Alejandro's bodega
     just before siesta
and the time the wine turned to vinegar
     and that Christmas mass when the priest died
     ...

...
It was all there
The winter shawl made by Maria Helena
for the statue of Our Lady
And the perfect olives grown by Tio Miguel
        on his dry and scorched huerto
All caught in the pulsing rhythms
        of blazing heels and castanets

Delilia consumed by Duende was danced
        by the joy the sorrow
        the pleasure the pain
        the sugar the lemon
        the life and the death
        the laugh and the scream
        the pain and the fire
Nothing escaped that pulsing dance

We could all die!
Santo Padre!
Death is near!

Then a sudden dark silence
        caught it all by the throat

Madre de Dios

Delilia's last step
        without remorse
        had smashed it all

And there on the bottom step
        no, not tonight
Death turned away
        from the singer's heart

No match for the Duende in the room
        the night Delilia danced
        flamenco

TURTLE DREAM

Why can't a turtle fly
   really like it did last night
      flying and gliding above
         the crowded ballroom floor

We swooped over the startled dancers
   far below as they pointed up
      with their jeweled fingers
        to my flying turtle
          with its glistening
            cloisonné carapace

Clinging to his geometric back
   the shell grew hot
      as we moved lower
        gliding in slow tilting circles
          to the marbled inlaid floor

Calmly and deliberately
   he blew out his turtle breath
      turtle breath of green vapor
        smelling of fresh sage and the sea

Through the green mist
   gold French doors opened
      to the moon lit garden
      and ocean beyond

...

...
The dancers now in silk brocade pajamas
    dropped their necklaces
        in a mound as they swayed
            onto the grass

Flying through the door it was so easy then
    to roll off his glowing back
        and walk gracefully in the mist
        to the strains of a lullaby

Just above the
    now sleeping dancers
        resting quietly
            in the seaweed and the grass

GARDENER'S REMORSE

The garden looked better with that plant gone.
I had pulled the twisted thing up
roots and all were now in the street.
It was just all wrong I thought
wrong really wrong from the very first day.

I had searched and shopped for the scrubby thing
A plant perfect for the drought, the salesman said,
slow growing, light or shade, hardy in all climates,
can withstand high heat and low water.

It wasn't attractive that first day but those were dry times
in '88 in my few square feet of California.

Like an arranged marriage, I might learn to love
this strange cross between a mutant bonsai cypress
and a poison berry bush from a Disney cartoon.

Three drought years had gone by
and one blessed wet one
and that miserable plant still occupied
its almost hallowed ground in my garden.
It seemed an unwelcome peace keeper
separating the exploding South African gazanias
from the radiant Icelandic poppies.

If it weren't for its minuscule faded pink blossoms,
pink like the tiny shy flowers on an old doll's dress
and if it weren't for its miniature berries,
that even the sparrows avoided
...

...
And if it weren't for its seeds looking like crushed
wheat germ kernels on the kitchen floor,
I'd say the ugly thing was dead and hadn't
moved a cell in four years. Slow growing?
Well, I guess!

I pulled the damn thing up without a tinge
of remorse. Good riddance I thought,
to be done with old ugly.
The next day, pondering the cleared spot
in the garden, I swear I heard my mother's voice
a voice long gone but still cajoling...

Oh, Dougie, you pulled up a slow growing plant.
How would you like it if someone did that to you?

Noah's Other Ark

The Ark of The Noah Project
crafted from dreams of redwood trees
carries below its groaning decks
carefully stored in the scent of cedar
treasure chests of ancient sounds
long held sacred
in the hearts of men

The figurehead of this Ark
that never goes to shore
some say is a dark angel
with open mouth and great blue wings
carrying in his strong carved hands
a basket of sweet vowels
and tangy consonants picked
from trees that grew by temple gates
in a country now below waves

Crewed by brothers of song
kind men of good will singing
the ark drifts calmly
through the haze of night
on a gently rocking sea

On the open deck
of redwood dreams
beside an open chest
open men with up raised faces
gently send to the star bright sky
their breath, their love, their songs

THOSE BUCKEYES

Oh, lord, lord, lord, it's terrible
        as Neruda had his precious socks
        I have my delicious buckeyes
        thirty-six hand carried from Texas
        and now the bowl is nearly empty

Just two precious morsels remain
        that celebrate the perfect wedding
        of chocolate and peanut butter

They are so beautiful
        on the highest shelf
        in the refrigerator
        their crystal container
        lording it over the
        pickles and chutney

Over time, each bite
        has been a ritual, a sacrament
        a celebration of gratitude

The miraculous, the divine
        caught for a moment
        in my mouth

I've never felt worthy of their deliciousness
        I confess that's painfully true
        I'm merely mortal after all

...

...

On that fearsome and dreaded day
　　　when the crystal bowl is empty
　　　may my sobs and tears be a testament
　　　that for a few blissful moments
　　　in this pedestrian world
　　　I have been abundantly blessed

I have had buckeyes
I have had buckeyes

GRATITUDE GOULASH – a recipe

Take down your biggest pot
> bigger than you think you need

Slice, dice or cut into manageable pieces
> memories of unbounded joy
> and the desiccated remains
> of life's calamitous events

Now throw them in the pot

Look around for missed ingredients
> there are bound to be some

Add spring water, local honey, vinegar,
> a pinch of heaven
> a smidgen of hell

Bring this mess to a rolling boil, cover, reduce heat
> simmer on a back burner for
> as long as it takes
> stirring occasionally

When your kitchen has a mysterious scent
> ask a close friend to dinner

Get out a couple bowls
> they need not match

...

...
Just before serving fold in
a cup of success
and a quarter pound of failure

Then be very liberal with paprika
this is goulash after all

Welcome your friend to the table
solemnly bless what's there
taste the bitter and the sweet

One bite is all you'll need
enough to taste
the complex flavors of gratitude

Now forget the goulash
take your friend out to dinner

Order something you've never tried

& 44

POETRY BODY & FENDER REPAIR

The sign said, **Poetry Body & Fender Repair**
In smaller print <u>Domestic Only</u>
and even smaller print
Experienced English Major on Duty

My dented poem about lost youth and food coloring
had a few problems so I pushed it in the open door

"May we be of service, sir?"
My poem has a slow leak and now and then the steering is
loose

"That's dreadful. Have you discerned
anything else, sir?"
Well, it starts ok but it slows down
when I change directions

"Has it been repaired before, sir?"
Too many times I'm afraid

"Sir, it appears your poem has met with a collision."
How can you tell?

"There is a plethora of indications. We can hear
a whispering murmur, a susurrus actually
from under the hood. And it's dripping verbs at an appalling
rate."

Plethora? Susurrus? Appalling? I don't use words
like that.

"There you have it. That's your problem sir.
Good day."

SENIOR DISCOUNT TUESDAY

I was at **Ross *Dress For Less*** yesterday.
Senior Discount Tuesday
buying a new set of sweats

Middle aged Chinese clerk: Are you 55?
Me: (shrugging) Oh, my yes.

Clerk: May I see your I.D.?
Me: (bug-eyed) You're kidding!

Clerk: (cold stare) How old are you?
Me: (humbly) I'm 84.

Clerk: Please, may I see your I.D.?
      (she looks)

Clerk: Oh my God. You are old!
Me: (laughing) Thanks. You've made my day.

Clerk: (nodding) You are 80 and alive.
Me: (insistent) No, I'm 84.

Clerk: Let me see license again.
Me: 1932. That means I'm 84.

Clerk: Oh my God. You are alive long time.
Me: Let's see if I'm around next Tuesday.

Clerk: Be very careful.
True story.

Waving Good-Bye

A new suitcase in one hand
car keys in the other and finally
off to college for the first time

Looking back past the walnut tree
a last glance at the old house
his family still waving good-bye
good-bye from behind
the screened-in porch

Shifting gears on Main Street,
thinking of things left behind
his old room and a medal from track
closet full of memories and old clothes
all still too good
to give away

Homecoming for the Thanksgiving feast
stunned at the barrenness of his room
just one change of socks and underwear remaining
in the top right drawer of the otherwise
empty chest

Staring down the hallway at Christmas,
past the presents and the lighted tree
he saw his room was gone
the doorway and the door
across from his brother's room
...

...
At spring break under the walnut tree
staring again at the screened-in porch
he was certain
the house was gone

Trying one last time in June
the porch was gone
the tree was gone
Main Street nowhere
to be found

Driving away past his disappearing high school
he wondered was there a medal from track
Had he ever had a brother

Clutching the wheel in front
he knew he must hurry
his road disappearing
his town disappearing
and in the rear view mirror

was that his life

slowly waving

good-bye, good-bye

CLEANING Up After The Poetry Salon

It's not always easy
    proper nouns are manageable
      they stack well for easy hauling
Biggest on the bottom
    The Great Plains, Idaho, Mt. Shasta
      then the smaller stuff left behind
        boxcars, photographs, you know

Adjectives are remarkably tough to clean up
The dry ones catch on the furniture
    bury themselves in cracks
      hide in the pocket of an old sweater
They crumble to awkward, ungainly,
    unmanageable, yes fragile pieces
      that cunningly avoid the shedding broom
       some careless poet has left behind
And wet ones like sticky and slimy - yikes!

Cleaning up the leavings of Wendell Berry?
    it's a grange meeting hall
Rich black dirt everywhere
    corn stalks, the lingering thick odor of
      compost and just a hint of cow manure
      on your shoes and your best carpet!

And Jesus! Those poems about stars
    the poets have no idea
      whole constellations left behind
       watch it with Ursa Major, its claws are sharp
        and a warning, the Seven Sisters keep coming back
  ...

...

My rule would be
    you brought 'em, you take 'em home

Food is good in a poem
    Mom's apple pie and romantic dinners for two
    are easily consumed by the salon - no leftovers
It's the ethnic dishes with strange names
    lutefisk, sauerkraut, gefilte fish
      and anything made with hot peppers
Well, you know

And come on, no animals bigger
    than a cat or small dog,
      polar bears and coyotes are disasters

Oh, I could go on
    mixed metaphors sliding
      down the walls and tangled
        in the drapes

Cliches hiding their heads in the corners
    embarrassed squirrels standing by dead seals
      stinking sea weed and sharks behind the sofa
      and fish - fish beyond number
        flopping on the floor

Verbs are easy, they move around
    just open a door and they
      take care of themselves

But poets,
  It's the birds left behind
    egret, robin, wrens, a flock of seagulls,
      a murder of crows
For God's sake leave a window open
...

& 50

...
But eagle, oh my friends, the eagle
   he glowers there
      from the chandelier
Righteously indignant
   a moment in a poem
      then forgotten
         in the closed room

I know, I know
   I'm making a new mess now
      I'll need some help here with
         the gefilte fish and that eagle

For the rest
   I brought 'em,
      I'll take 'em home

&STUFF

One man's junk is another man's stuff
     Hold my stuff and watch this
That stuff is heavier than it looks
     There is old stuff no one talks about
He knocked the stuff out of that guy
     Some stuff doesn't have a name
Oh, he was made of sterner stuff
     There is stuff that happens to other people
Just stuff your stuff behind the couch
     Well, in the end it's my stuff to sort out

What the hell is all this stuff about stuff
     Are you serious with this stuff?

*"So, dear reader, you've made it to my stuff pages. You know how it is when you clean the garage or basement and find stuff that for some reason you couldn't throw away? Well, here is some stuff from the drawer marked **"LIFE BUOYS"** and some stuff from the box labeled **"SWAN BOATS."** You're welcome to any of this stuff."*
-DvK

A Murder Of Crows

So today, on a cold January morning, I was riding my bike around the lower circle of the polo fields in Golden Gate Park. I was on my third loop around and going like hell to get over to the sunny side of the track once again. There were no other bikers. No speed skaters on roller blades. No elderly tai-chi practitioners moving like willows in the wind. I didn't even see a gardener or a homeless person and that's unusual.

It was only me, a cloudless blue sky and the brilliant green grass in the great field where Saturday soccer games are played. And *"then what to my wondering eyes should appear"* above the eastern end of the field but a moving black cloud. So wondrous I had to stop in the shade.

Like a flotilla of stealth bombers, hundreds of crows were coming in for a landing. Once on the ground they began waddling around like some huge geriatric drill team waiting for the parade to begin. They became two hundred or more guys in tuxedos waiting for drinks before the ball room doors opened for the banquet. Too fat from a good winter but ready to chow down while waiting for the key note speaker to begin.

It could have been the survivor's reunion of the 247th Nest Defense Brigade or the regional meeting of the Royal Order of the Mystic Keepers of Sound and Fury.

One old guy with a torn sleeve was going from group to group, really giving them hell.

"I know I told you. Damn it, I told you at the board meeting. What the hell's with you guys? We keep our agreements. We were supposed to have a by-laws meeting last night! Hey, you there Charley! You knew about it cuz I called you. You were gonna tell...Gonna tell... Ah, jeez, now I forgot who you were gonna tell but what the hell's with you guys?" And he was off again on another harangue about the economy or maybe it was the war.

I watched one of the old birds who walked like a candidate for a hip replacement, make a bee line for the bar.

I guess they ran out of booze just then because the place exploded with rage. Imagine two hundred angry and raucous crows. There was then some sort of signal only they knew. Like a black blanket shaking itself in the cold they became airborne. And fast as anything, the Royal Order of the Mystic Keepers of Sound and Fury were gone.

The Bully In The Garden

It was a beautiful day in the Garden of Delight. It was the first day of spring. The colors were magnificent.

All the children from throughout the land had come to play together in the Garden of Delight. The children were like flowers. They all wore clothing from their home village. There were children with long flowered skirts and others with orange sarongs. There were long pants and short pants and overalls and some were almost bare. Some had high boots, some had sandals and some had no shoes at all. Every language in the world was spoken by the children in the Garden of Delight. They didn't speak alike and they didn't look alike either. It was marvelous.

If they couldn't understand one another's speech, it made no difference. They didn't need words to be together. They helped each other without words. If they messed up something, they laughed together and tried again. When they were tired they lay down and napped together. No one paid attention to the differences and distinctions that could have divided them. They drank the same water, they breathed the same air and when they cried their tears tasted the same.

Wait. Why would there be tears in The Garden of Delight?

Well, as it sometimes happens, a Bully with a Red Hat from a tall tower in the East came stamping into the Garden. The way he behaved you might have thought he owned the Garden! Since everything foreign and strange made him afraid, he tried to make all the children afraid of each other.

And he bragged and lied about how strong he was. He told the children they were stupid if they didn't believe him. The Garden was in trouble, big trouble. He would fix it. He said he was going to take over the Garden and throw everyone out that didn't walk and talk and think like they did. And once he got rid of everyone who was different, he'd build a wall around the Garden and keep them out!

Well the children stopped playing and looked at each other. Some couldn't understand his words but they knew the Bully with the Red Hat from the Tower in the East was talking about them. And they thought it was funny. How could he throw out everyone who was different? There would be nobody left! They thought it was funny. And they laughed.

And they laughed louder and louder until the narcissistic ego maniac with delusions of grandeur couldn't hear his own hateful speech. How could they laugh at him? He was perfect. He snarled at the laughing children and ran from the Garden.

And what of the children? What did they do? They hugged each other and in several languages said something like, "Boy, that was a close call. He might have made it happen. Then where would we be?"

No one knows where the Bully with the Red Hat went when he left the garden. They say he's still around. Have you seen him?

$\mathcal{G}$IVE $\mathcal{M}$E $\mathcal{A}$ "$\mathcal{Z}$"

OK. It's a fantasy but I can imagine it so clearly. The box of letters is huge. So huge it has to sit in the driveway. No, not those hand written letters that come in the mail. I'm talking letters like "D" and "R" and "Y's" and they are mixed in the box in all sizes and colors and styles. A *Times New Roman* "F" sits on a *Copperplate* "B" on top of a *Harrington* "M" and there are hundreds and hundreds of letters in the box. And they are big. It might take two hands to pick up an "M". Do you get the picture?

See, I'm teaching a young boy to read. He tells me his letters won't stay still on the page. They slide off the page into his lap or somewhere. His shoulders droop as he tells me his eyes can't make them stay next to each other.

So together we climb up the side and lower ourselves into the box. Wow. I'm impressed and the boy's eyes are huge. "What do you think young fellow? Can you find a "C"? Look for an "O" with a bite out of the side."

He starts digging. "You're getting close, that's a "Q" because it's got a tail. Hey, there you go. You've got yourself a "C" and it's a big one."

I say, "Should we make a word? Not too big a word now, because these letters might get heavy. Pick a word and we'll give it a go." We're silent for a bit. "Come on. Huh? Zebra? You want to spell Zebra? Why on earth do you want Zebra? How about Cat or Bat or Fat?" Nope. He wants Zebra and now I do too. Well why not? "OK. OK. Zebra it is."

I use my big finger to draw a picture of a "Z" onto his little palm. He gets it. He draws a "Z" on my palm with a small positive finger. "Yeah. Let's go!" So together we dig in the box, a box big as a dumpster.

The letters fly and he goes wild. "What's this?" he yells from a corner. I yell back "that's an "N" leave it there!" "But it looks like a Z." "Nah, keep looking." And so it goes. I get my foot tangled in a pile of *Curlz* but we soldier on.

"Yea." he shouts. He's found them all and letter by letter I shout out, "give me a "Z!" He lays down a one pound *Noteworthy* "Z." "Give me an "E!"

He sets down a white plastic *Herculanum* "E." Give me a "B!" And with his two small hands he lays them all in front of his scuffed brown shoes. ZEBRA. And the word doesn't slide away or get tangled. In fact, it seems to glow.

He joins the ZEBRA later with a RObIN and a CoYOTE. Now tired, he smiles and carefully, letter by letter up the side of the box, he spells out LADDER. He is so proud and I am too. And together we climb up the ladder, one letter at a time.

Now give me a "Jî!" Give me an "O!" Give me a "Y!"

MEDITATION ON ADMIRATION
IN THE VICTORIAN MODE

It is so fine to be admired. Can anything really compare? And the admiration from a younger man is surely the best. The most perfect sunrise must come in second. To bask in the soft and slightly tearful warmth of admiration's un-judgmental outpouring is to be truly seen, but I fear, not known.

If he knew me would the admiration come so fully? Oh, I know what he must be seeing. It is all there, the grey hair, the lines writing messages of hope on my face, the eyes of mine that have such belief in youth and beauty. But that other part of him (perhaps unknown to his waking mind) sees the uncle or father or grandfather he is missing and needs like fresh air. And that is all fine by me, this feeling.

Is there really anything better to do than just be there for someone like a chair or a warm sweater? Perhaps I'm just a little further down the road he hopes to travel. Who knows?

I cannot dismiss, however, the sweetness of that gaze that was before me, and how deeply I felt the love. For in the moment of admiring that was the all and everything between us. Love. Just love, one man looking at another man and experiencing love. But then, his courage, because what was felt was said, I heard him say it, "I Love you, Doug." Just that. I love you, Doug. Then I could say to him what I had wanted to speak for so long, "I love you too."

He blessed me that day with his admiration and I blessed him the same and more with mine. It was not hard for I have much to notice well of him.

Well he carries himself, this young responsible worker. His rolling walk says someone is happily at home inside. Oh, and he loves to sing and his songs become a window to his moods. And he is quick to laugh and is strongly fierce in his loyalties.

But what fills me with unbounded delight is the sheer wholeness of him. He is a young man, finished with a high education and he is not shut down or numb. His emotions flow full and his mind can dance with imaginary things and very real ideas. There is much to admire in him and I have told him so.

I wonder if he believes me, or like I, he thinks, "Oh, if he really knew me, he would not be so kind."

Swan Boats On Lake Clinton

January 4, 2014

Dear Family and Friends,

My annual letter is a little late but it has been quite a year. Some of you remember we had an earthquake on the San Andreas Fault last September while I was out of town in Minnesota and that I had to buy a Zodiac inflatable to get back to my otherwise undisturbed home? I still feel like Jacque Cousteau every time I go for groceries. San Francisco, the city that used to "know how," has abandoned all attempts to drain the lake that has formed in front on my home. Or did you know it wiped out six city blocks just across from my house? Talk about a sink hole!

Who knew there were three sizable springs flowing underground from Mt. Davidson to Stow Lake in Golden Gate Park! I now live on lake front property. I was delighted however that the city fathers are turning it into a park. I have been granted the Swan Boat concession. The short pier already extends out into the lake. Seagulls have arrived to poop on it, but I have plans for a seagull fillet brunch on Sundays served off the pier so it will hopefully all work out.

So now I await springtime tourists and the swan shaped paddle boats being built across the bay in Alameda. I hope to have several jobs earmarked for the boys of Troup 69, the Gay Sea Scouts from the Castro. They can earn merit badges teaching water safety and engaging in humane raccoon trapping while renting out the paddle boats.

Speaking of things Gay, I'm working on a nefarious scheme to raise the consciences' of non-gay Mormons when they approach my pier. If they want to rent a boat they have to sign a petition for a referendum making it legal for Mormons to marry and live in California but if they have children they have to leave. I think I'll have the scouts collect the signatures carrying rainbow clip boards which will cleverly match their rainbow speedos. I know I'm being petty, but have I ever been less than? But I digress. Somehow the raccoon population is expanding around the lake along with possums and, of all things, coyotes. I plan to ship them to Fargo, North Dakota by Fed Ex.

& 62

There was some other good news. St. Cecilia's, the church that used to be down the street but is now across the lake, escaped the quake. Well not totally, the spire has a strange tilt, but they attributed its non-collapse to the new pope and his new slant on Catholicism so it's all cool. Right?

Attendance has picked up and Confirmation Sunday was a delight to witness with the canoes being paddled to church by little boys and girls in white. It was such a blessing to observe the parade across the water from my pier.

Perhaps I can have a priest from St. Cecilia's come and bless my Swan Boats the same day they bless the neighbor's cats, dogs and chickens.

I thought of opening a designer coffee shop in my basement but since there are already 4,327 places to buy a latte in San Francisco I'll keep my options open. My next door neighbor beat me to a muffin, croissant and T-Shirt shop so I'll see what develops. We're trying to establish a world free trade area here on Lake Clinton. Too bad the world is now digital, because I could make a fortune selling film to tourists.

Along with my other civic duties last year, I served on the Mayor's Street Naming Commission. I've since resigned.

There was just too much stress over renaming Grant Avenue, which runs through the center of Chinatown to Governor Arnold Schwarzenegger Boulevard. It wasn't the huge size of the new signage to accommodate the name that was the problem but how to translate the street signs to Chinese. Seems Schwarzenegger lost a lot in translation. Pagoda Drive was a non-starter. My suggestion of Terminator Drive was rejected. And my idea to wait and name the street Brown Avenue in honor of our present Governor was shouted down. I could not stand the acrimony so I wished them well and resigned.

I'll have plenty to do launching my little fleet of Swan Boats without having all of my careful efforts at political correctness disregarded and demeaned.

& 63

Well, dear family and friends, that's all the good news. Have a great year.

Next time you're in town come visit *Old Uncle Doug's Party Pier* on the balmy shores of Lake Clinton. We'll be open 10 to 4 any sunny day. The scouts and I will be glad to see you.

See you soon,

Uncle Doug

Swan Boat Rides

At Old Uncle Doug's Party Pier

Lake Clinton Park - San Francisco

10am to 4pm every sunny day

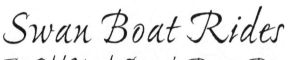

Allow the bearer <u>20 Minute</u> free ride on

The Golden Cygnet

(not valid on Sundays or Holidays)

Made in United States
North Haven, CT
02 September 2023

41046132R00039